Copyright © 2021 by Tracey D'Amore
Published and distributed in the United States by

All rights reserved. This book or any portion thereof may not be
reproduced or used in any manner whatsoever without the express
written permission of the publisher except for the use of brief quotations
in a book review.

ISBN: 978-1-7363649-3-2
Printed in the United States of America

THE MIND OF A MILITARY MOM

TIPS AND ADVICE ON HOW TO SURVIVE THE JOURNEY

written by

TRACEY D'AMORE

AUTHORS NOTE

The Mind of A Military Mom will shed light on my experience and what I went through when both of my boys joined the Military. Myself, as well as other Military Moms, offer advice and tips on how to survive the Military Mom journey. A special thank you to all of the moms who were thoughtful enough to contribute their precious advice. Their names, as well as the names of my 2 boys, have been changed for their privacy. I would also like to thank Anthony A.J. Joiner and his publishing company for the creation of this book, along with everyone else that played a part in making this book a reality.

You will notice throughout the book that the words "Military Mom(s)" is capitalized. I feel that All Military Moms deserve honor and respect... No further explanation needed!

DEDICATION

I am dedicating this book to my two boys. If it weren't for them, this book would not exist. Words cannot express how proud I am of them both. They will forever be my heroes! I wish them a lifetime of good health, happiness, and God's Grace. I love you both, always and forever!

CONTENTS

Introduction 01
My Story 02-18
Interview
    Questions 1 and 2 19
    Question 3 23
    Question 4 26
    Question 5 29
Advice For New Veteran Military Moms 35
    Communication 36
    Love/Prayers/Support 37
    Sacrifice & Strenght 38
    Pride/Self-Reflection/Gratitude 39
    Family and Friends 40
    Education 42
About the Author 48
Support 49
Apparel 50

INTRODUCTION

When our children took the oath to serve our great country, so did we! We suddenly went from being an average mom, to a Military Mom. Our new title brought us many new questions, concerns, fears, sacrifices, and emotions...emotions we probably never even knew we were capable of feeling. *How am I going to survive this? What if something bad happens to my child? I'm scared, I'm worried. Is what I'm feeling normal?*

Being a Military Mom does not come with an owner's manual. We are left to figure this new role out on our own. This book was created so you don't have to figure it out on your own. *The Mind of A Military Mom* is here to help you when you're questioning your feelings, and trying to survive your Military Mom journey. Let's do this together!

I remember it like it was yesterday. In my eyes, it was one of the worst days of my life. I was sitting on my loveseat and Joe, my son, was sitting on the couch. It was the middle of summer. It was just the two of us having our normal conversations about hockey and everyday life, while we were watching TV and playing on our phones. At one point, the conversation had stopped, as both of us had our heads buried in our phones. Then, out of the blue, there it was...those dreaded words that no mother ever wants to hear her child say. "Mom, I think I want to join the Military." I set my phone down on the couch. My heart just about stopped beating, and I felt all my blood draining from my head and face. I looked at Joe and said, "You want to do what???" He said, "I've been thinking about it, and I want to join the Military." I just stared at him, speechless for a couple of seconds and said, "Why, why would you want to do that? What branch?" His response was both admirable and heart-wrenching! "The Marines. I want to be in Infantry so I can fight for our country, and put an end to ISIS and other terrorist groups." At the time, ISIS was a big problem for our country. As my eyes filled with tears, I asked him when and what made him come to this decision. He told me that he had been thinking about it for about a year. I was completely numb, and like any or most moms, I tried to talk him out of it. I gave him every possible bad scenario I could think of...losing a limb, losing his hearing, losing his eye sight, PTSD, mental issues later on in life, possibly not being able to play with his children someday, and the worst of them all - Death! I tried to explain to him that it's not Play Station...there is no second or third chance! You name it, I tried absolutely everything to get him to change his mind. Everything! When I was all finished with my speech, his response was, "I know

Mom, I'll be fine." My eyes filled with tears again, and I told him I needed to think about it, and that I wasn't too happy about it. He said he understood why I felt that way, but he had put a lot of thought into it and that's what he wants to do. I had just aged five years because of his persistence and determination to enlist. He went on to tell me that if he pre-enlisted by the end of August (as a Poolee), he would be able to train/workout at the Base gym. This would benefit him because he would get into good shape before entering boot camp.

    I understood his reasoning behind it, but that would mean he would be the property of the USMC while he was still in high school! So many thoughts went through my head (again). What if his father and I let him enlist early and then he changed his mind before he graduated from high school? There were no "take-backs"… he would be stuck with his decision and would be the property of the U.S. Marine Corps. As a mom, the thought of my seventeen-year-old son being the property of the Marine Corps did not sit well with me at all. After many painful conversations, his father and I decided to sign the papers for him to pre-enlist. We knew Joe was determined and confident in his decision to become a Marine, and if we didn't sign those papers, he would have enlisted when he turned eighteen anyway. Either way, we lost that battle. As much as I didn't want my son to do this, I wanted him to be as ready and prepared as he possibly could be before entering boot camp. On August 9, 2016, we signed the enlistment papers. Needless to say, Joe was very happy, and I was sick to my stomach! *What did I just do? Why did I do this to myself?* Those questions were swimming around in my head for weeks after I signed those papers.

Joe had started training at the Base gym, received his Poolee t-shirt, and was on his way to becoming a United States Marine. His senior year of high school had started, and life went on as normal. Soon after that, it was hockey season and Joe was playing his last year of high school hockey. I was happy it was hockey season again because it gave my mind a break from thinking about what was to come for my son at the end of graduation. During the beginning stages of his pre-enlistment, we had a couple of meetings with his recruiting Sergeant. He came to the house to discuss what and how everything was going to work, and Joe received his little box with all that "stuff" they give to the new recruits. Again, I was sick to my stomach. *Did I do the right thing by signing those papers?* Joe was excited and very proud of himself, and was ready to memorize all that was required of him...and so he did that. The year was going by at an extremely fast pace (so it seemed). I was praying for time to slow down, as I did not want high school graduation to get here. Unfortunately, time doesn't stand still. Hockey season was coming to an end. As in any high school sport, there was Senior Night. Parents were escorted out on the ice by their son, while an announcer said their name and their plans for after graduation. When Joe's name was called, and the announcer said that he had pre-enlisted in the Marine Corps, the crowd stood on their feet and gave him a standing ovation! Wow, what a feeling that was for me as his mom! I am sure Joe felt the love and pride too. I was so beyond proud of my son. Don't get me wrong, as much as I didn't want my son to join the Military, I was extremely proud of him for being so courageous and wanting to do such an admirable thing...something that not every teenage boy is cut out to do. So, fast forward a little and here we were at the end of the school year. It was time for graduation. All graduates who had enlisted in the Military wore a different color sash than the other graduates. During the ceremony, they honored these graduates by announcing their names and having them stand up (my son was one of four graduates who enlisted). There was a huge round of applause, and once again, tears filled my eyes, and pride came over my whole body! What an experience! Graduation had come and gone, and now it was just a waiting game for July 24, 2017. This was the day that Joe had to leave for boot camp. There were so many emotions felt by the whole family during those three weeks. I saw the stress start to come over Joe, as he realized time was closing in on him. His life, as well as mine, was about to change. Those three weeks had come to an end, and that dreaded day (for me) had come. Joe said his goodbyes to his brother and the rest of the family, and we were off to MEPS. It was a quiet ride with very little conversation (understandably so!). I knew my son was as scared as I was. Upon arriving at MEPS, Joe had to go through some finalities and the final swearing in. I have never seen such a stressed-out look on my son's face in all my life. The look on his face made me more scared than I had been already! I wanted to break down, grab my son, and leave... more like run out of there. Once the swearing-in ceremony was over, the recruits got to say their goodbyes to their families. Joe's girlfriend (now wife), myself, and Joe's dad were all there. We said our goodbyes with hugs (long hugs) and kisses. Needless to say, I cried my eyes out.

My baby was being taken away from me, he was only eighteen years old! I felt like I was having an out-of-body experience...that's how numb I was. I was scared for him and me. How were we going to get through this? I had never felt a fear like I did that day. It was now a waiting game for the phone call that every mom waits for...the call from your child telling you that he made it to Paris Island. When I got Joe's phone call, I could barely understand him because he was screaming so loud. It didn't even sound like my son. What a relieving, yet heart-wrenching phone call. I was so happy that he made it there safely, but I knew the hell he was about to go through would soon begin! I knew I wouldn't be receiving a letter from him for weeks. I would have to just wait. When I finally did get a letter from Joe, I was excited, happy, sad, and scared to open it. I was afraid of what it was going to say. As I expected, I cried when I read it, and I did the same with each and every letter he sent me. Those thirteen weeks were the longest thirteen weeks of my life, and the toughest!

Every day I wondered if Joe was eating good, and if he was physically and mentally healthy. I went through each day feeling worried, nervous, and scared for my son. I felt like I was living someone else's life. It was awful and unexplainable. I prayed, and I prayed a lot—it helped because I knew God would watch over my baby when I couldn't. Every day of those thirteen weeks was a struggle for me, but I pushed through because I knew my son was going through so much more than I was. Yes, I was worried, scared, and nervous, but he had to physically, mentally, and emotionally endure so much more than me. This was especially true when he had entered the Crucible. The Crucible is the final test and the culmination of everything a recruit learns and works for during the thirteen weeks of boot camp. It was 54 hours long: 45 miles of hiking, 45 pounds of gear, 36 warrior stations, 29 team-building exercises, and all with only 6 hours of sleep and 2 MRE's (meals ready to eat). This is the part that every mom fears and loses sleep over. I was happy that it was time for the Crucible, and scared at the same time.

I was happy because it meant that it was the end of boot camp and my son would become a Marine. However, I was scared because I knew he was going to go through hell and experience the hardest thing in his life. As a Marine Mom in the making, I too had prepared myself for the Crucible. I bought and customized a special Crucible lantern, decorated some candles, made some signs, and turned a designated area into a Crucible shrine for my son. This was very special to me, and I cherished it. Aside from that, it kept me inspired and hopeful that my son was going to get through this and become a United States Marine. I had two sleepless nights filled with worry and fear, but it was worth it. Joe had made it through the Crucible and became a United States Marine! It was now time for his graduation... Finally! Graduation at Paris Island, South Carolina was an unbelievable and unforgettable experience. My family and I watched the Motto Run, spent time with Joe on Family Day, and watched the Graduation ceremony.

Family Day started with the Motto Run. The Motto Run was such a spectacular sight to see. Families lined the streets of Paris Island with signs, flags, and t-shirts that read "Marines," or their son's or daughter's platoon number. We watched our sons and daughters run in formation with their platoons down the Paris Island streets, carrying their platoon flag. Everyone cheered as these Marines ran by. You could actually feel the pride all around you from the moms and families that were there. It was absolutely breathtaking, and something I will never forget. After the Motto Run was the formal ceremony. Basically, the Marine Corps holds this ceremony to announce to the families (before they release them to us), that these men and women were now U.S. Marines. Once the ceremony ended, families were allowed to go onto the platform, find their Marine, and spend time with them until 3:00 pm. As soon as the Marines fell out of formation, my family and I made our way down to the platform as fast as we could.

Frantically, I searched for my son. I couldn't wait any longer to wrap my arms around my baby! The crowd made it very difficult to locate him – there were people and Marines everywhere. All of a sudden, I hear "Mom." I turned and looked, and there was this Marine standing there. He was smiling. I just stared – probably for about a few seconds, which is a really long time. It was my son! That boy that I sent off to boot camp thirteen weeks ago had turned into a man. Wow, this is so emotional for me to write about this... it takes me right back to that day! I hugged my son so hard as I bawled my eyes out. I didn't want to let him go. There wasn't one mom there who wasn't crying! All of these poor moms hadn't seen their babies, or hugged and kissed them in thirteen weeks. What torture that is for a mother. I was lucky enough that a Paris Island photographer captured a beautiful picture of me hugging my son. They even put it in one of their graduation newsletters. What a proud and honorable moment for me. It was now time for Graduation. There is so much I can say about it, but I would not do it justice. I will say that there is nothing like it, and I have never felt so much admiration and pride in all my life.

I cried tears of joy and pride, all the while thinking: "Wow, I can't believe my baby is a United States Marine!" When all was said and done, it was time to take my Marine home on leave, at least for a little while. It was a gut-wrenching time in my life, but in the end, it didn't and still doesn't compare to the pride, admiration, and respect that I have for my son...my Marine, my hero!

But wait! This is not the end of my story. Fast forward to 2018, and I am standing in my kitchen. In walks my older son, John. John was 22 years old at the time, and had a state job. I was cleaning up the kitchen when he came through the door. We started sharing how each of our days were, and then he blind-sided me and says, "I think I'm going to join the Military." Once again, my heart stopped beating. I selfishly thought, "Oh no, I can't go through this again!"

After hearing him say that, my stress started to subside a little. We continued to talk about it, and even though I was somewhat at ease with his decision, I still had to give him "the talk" about what he would go through. I had to let him know that B.M.T. (Basic Military Training) would not be easy, and was he really ready to go through all of that? Afterall, he knew what his brother went through in boot camp. Just as I did with Joe, as a mom, it was my job to educate and protect my sons to the best of my ability, and let them know that once you decide to join the Military and sign those papers...there's no turning back. You are the property of the United States Air Force! John assured me that he knew what he was going to have to go through, and this was what he really wanted to do. The more we talked and the more I got to process it, I was happy that he chose this career path. I was, of course, very proud of him and relieved that he decided what direction he wanted to go in.

However, I have to say, I walked around beaming with pride… I have two kids in the Military, not many people can say that. I guess for me, this was such a great accomplishment as a mom. Moms are always proud of their kids but come on, this is the United States Military… The world's best! The four-and-a-half months had passed, and it was time for John to leave for Basic Training. Here come all the emotions… AGAIN! I didn't want to send my son off to the Military. I was very sad, but I knew he had to go. We got in the car, and headed to the airport, which was about a 45-minute drive. I tried to hide my emotions and have a somewhat normal conversation, as I didn't want John to see how upset and sad I really was. I didn't want to contribute to the existing stress he most likely had about going into the unknown. Although he said he was ready for this, and anxious to get there, I knew deep down that he had to be feeling a little bit of fear.

When we arrived at the airport, John checked in at the desk. As the airport Attendant was entering his information, she said, "You better get going. This flight is about to take off. I will call the gate to see if they'll wait." My heart is beating fast as I write this because it feels like I am reliving it! John and I looked at each other with panic on our faces. I quickly kissed and hugged him goodbye, and told him that I loved him very much. He then took off running to catch his flight. I just stood there watching my son run down the airport hallway, and I broke down into tears! We didn't get to spend any time together in the airport before his flight, like I wanted to. I didn't get to tell him what I wanted to tell him…all those words of encouragement and how proud I was of him. Yeah, of course I told him all of this before, but I wanted to tell him again. I was upset about that, I was upset that he was leaving, and to top it all off, I was worried that he was going to miss his flight.

As I was leaving the airport, John texted to tell me he had made it on the plane. I was so relieved. Driving home from the airport, the tears continued to flow. All I could think about was how lonely it was going to be with both of my boys gone...*How was I going to survive this? What was life gonna be like not having both of my boys around to talk to, to laugh with, to hug, to kiss, and to make memories with?* I was not in a good mental place! Anyway, John had called me when he arrived at Lackland Air Force Base, telling me that he arrived safely and that he didn't know when he would be able to call again. He gave me his address and said he would write as often as he could. I was happy to hear his voice, and told him I loved him and was very proud of him. During his two months at basic training, I made sure I wrote to him once a week, just as I had with Joe. John wrote back as often as he could and was even able to call once in a while.

I looked forward to getting his letters, but I was also anxious. I was always afraid that I would open up one of his letters to him saying that it was awful and that he had made a mistake by joining. Thank God that wasn't the case. John had met some really nice guys, and got along with them quite well. As a matter of fact, he became somewhat of a leader to his fellow Airmen. John had started a tradition while in B.M.T. At the end of the day, he would try to keep everyone motivated and positive by saying to them, "Another Day Down Boys!" Apparently, the guys loved it and looked forward to him saying that everyday. Believe it or not, there were several Airmen that told me when I went to graduation that if it weren't for him saying that, they didn't know how they would make it through. Imagine that... one simple sentence was able to make a difference in the lives of these Airmen. When I heard about this, I was again filled with pride for my son! One of his very last letters to me, he had said that they were going to be starting BEAST Week the following week.

BEAST Week stands for Basic Expeditionary Airman Skills Training. This is the equivalent to the Crucible for the Marines, though not as brutal. It is considered the final test to become an Airman. It was a simulation where all the trainees put all their combat skills into practice. Although BEAST Week is considered as the least brutal testing of all of the branches, it is still mentally and physically challenging. I was stressed out thinking that my son had to go through it. I was relieved and so happy to find out that John had made it through BEAST Week... and did quite well! The time had finally arrived. It was time for graduation, thank God! All I could think about was that the worst part was over, and I now have two kids in the Military. Wow, just wow! So, I started planning my trip to San Antonio, Texas, and let me tell you, this was just as stressful as worrying about boot camp. I could probably write a book on just the "getting to graduation" fiasco that I went through – Unbelievable!

Ok, where do I start? I'll start with the flight to San Antonio, which was mid-November.

My flight landed at my first layover airport, which, in all honesty, I don't even remember the name of. It might have been in North Carolina. Anyway, it was only an hour layover which shouldn't have been bad. However, that hour turned into a three-hour layover because there were mechanical issues with the plane. Ugh! Now I'm in a panic because I'm thinking that I'm going to miss my connecting flight... which I did. *Are you kidding me right now!* So now I had to wait for them to put me on another plane that was heading to San Antonio, which was two hours later than my original flight. By the time I got to San Antonio, it was midnight. I went to the counter to get my rental car, and the guy who helped me told me I owed $100 (it was some kind of fee), so I gave him my debit card. He ran my card and said that I didn't have enough money in there. *What?!* That couldn't be right. I get direct deposit, and it was payday. I checked my account and my paycheck had not deposited yet. I couldn't figure out what the hell was wrong, and the guy behind the counter was not giving me that rental car without the $100 deposit.

I panicked. I called my son's father and asked if he could wire the money into my account. He said he would, but it would take hours before it cleared. OMG, now I'm totally in a panic! Come to find out, my check wasn't going to be deposited into my account until Friday because it was Veteran's Day on Monday, which means the check is always a day late on a holiday week. I had completely forgot about it being a holiday week. At this point, I was practically hyperventilating! I've had no sleep, having been up for over 24 hours, and now had to sleep in the airport on a bench until my money gets deposited into my account... And all this just to get my rental car! I was in tears! So many thoughts were going through my exhausted mind...*What if I'm late getting to John's graduation? What if I came all the way here and end up not being there for my son?* I was so scared and so upset. I prayed to God that I would make it to graduation on time.

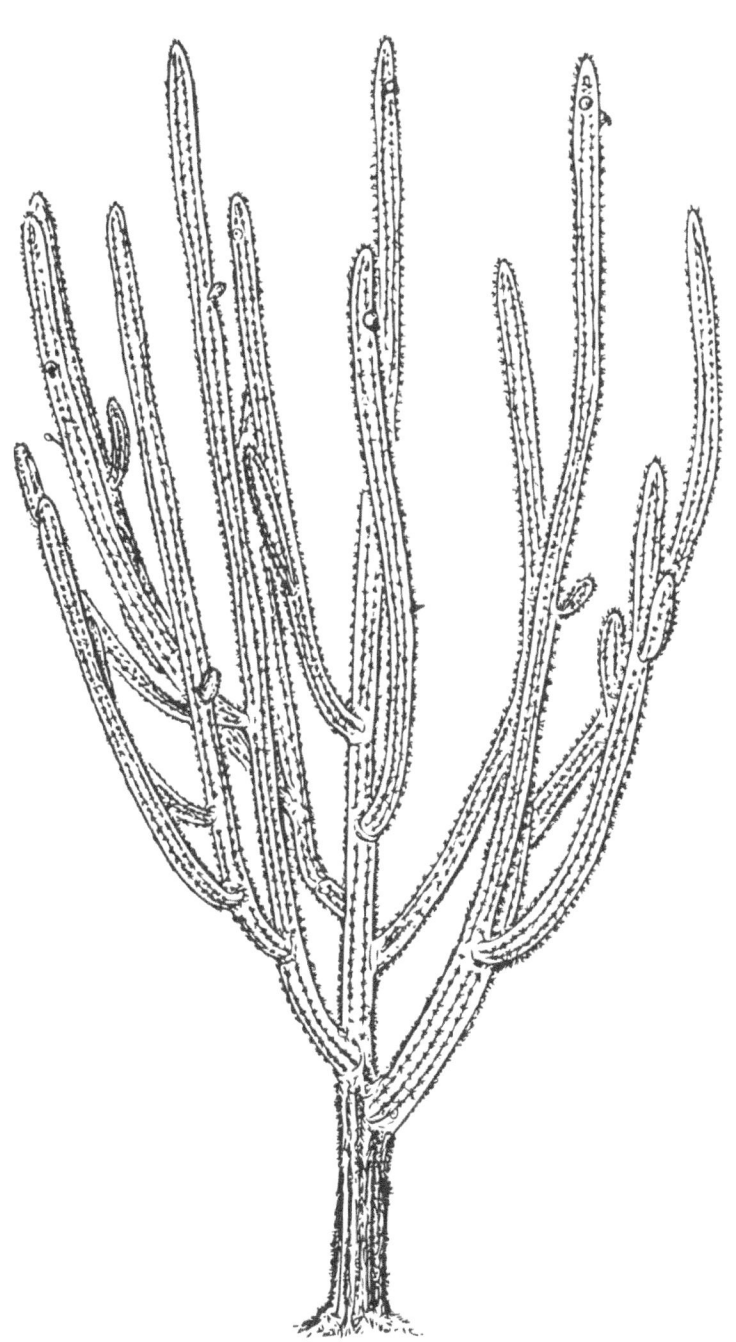

Morning came. I was not able to get any sleep in the airport (Gee, I wonder why), but the money was in my account. I got the rental car, drove as fast as I legally could to my hotel, showered, and was off to graduation. I made it on time, but with only minutes to spare... Thank you God! What a huge relief. The thought of my son graduating without me being there to see him literally made me sick to my stomach. The Air Force graduation ceremony was just as spectacular as the Marine's graduation ceremony. The Airmen were all standing in formation, separated by their flight numbers. There were families seated all around the platform that the Airmen were on... and for getting there just in time for the ceremony, I was able to get a seat on the bottom row. Once the ceremony was over, the families were able to go out on the platform and "Tap Out" their Airman!

"Tapping Out" is when a family member goes up to their Airman (while the Airman is still in formation, or at parade rest), and taps them on the shoulder or hugs them. Once an Airman is tapped out, he/she is free to go with their family. The platform, or parade deck, was filled with families looking for their Airman. I was lucky because it didn't take me long to find my son. When I found him, I hugged him so hard! It is so emotional for a mom when she gets to "tap out" her son/daughter... so many emotions go through your heart and head! I was relieved, proud, happy, excited, and on cloud nine! Never in a million years did I ever think that either of my boys would join the Military. We were officially a Military family. I was so proud of my son that words can't even begin to explain. So, John was tapped out, and it was time to take my son and spend some quality time with him in San Antonio.

First, he showed me around his barracks. I got to see where he slept, where his locker was, where his bathroom was, and where he ate. Obviously, it's a lot different than home! We then went to "The River." Wow, was that nice! I highly recommend you go there if you're ever in San Antonio. I've never seen anything like it. Absolutely gorgeous. When we went to the mall to get something to eat, John introduced me to some of his fellow Airman. What a great bunch of young men, so polite and respectful! This was an unforgettable experience to say the least, and I am so grateful that it all worked out in the end. Now, I was able to have my son home for a little while before he headed off to tech school. Thank you, God! Boot camps and Basic Trainings were now a thing of the past, and both of my boys were able to start their Military careers.

You might find this hard to believe, but the story (my story) that you just read, took many months to write. Why did it take me so long? Plain and simple, it was PAINFUL! Pain is what caused me to put the pen down and walk away. Pain is what I felt every time I began writing. Why? Because this was the most painful and gut-wrenching time of my life... Period! So many emotions I experienced on a daily basis changed me as a person, and changed the way I looked at life. You know, as well as I do, that being a mom puts you on a rollercoaster of emotions already as it is. Now, multiply that by 10 and add the emotions of fear, anxiety, loneliness, separation anxiety, and sadness when your sons join the Military. Every day I lived in a silent hell and hide my feelings, so it was difficult for me to rehash those feelings and put them into words.

However, there is no way that I was the only Military Mom feeling what I was feeling. I'm sure most, if not all Military Moms, were in that same or unique mindset that I was in. Well, I wanted to know. Not that I had to have my feelings validated, but because these emotions were so deep and personal, I wanted to know if this was all normal for a Military Mom to be experiencing. I decided to start a Facebook group called "Military Mom Life." I searched for other Military Moms and invited them to my group. I explained to them that this was a supportive and non-judgmental group where they could express their feelings, brag, and talk about anything that was on their hearts and minds. After all, only a Military Mom truly and deeply understands what another Military Mom is going through! I have had such great success with this group, and it is still going strong.

As I mentioned earlier, there were certain questions that I asked to a select group of Military Moms; five questions to be exact. The questions were: 1) What branch of the Military is your son/daughter in? 2) Explain what went through your mind when your son/daughter told you they wanted to join. 3) How has this changed your life? 4) What is your favorite part about being a Military Mom? 5) What is it like being a Military Mom?

I will start with the responses from question number two, only because most of these moms mention the Military branch their son/daughter is in throughout their interview. Let's dive in! These moms were asked to explain what went through their minds when their son/daughter told them they wanted to join, what their reaction was, and what emotions they felt.

INTERVIEW QUESTION 1 & 2

What Branch Of The Military Is Your Son/Daughter In? Explain What Went Through Your Mind When Your Son/Daughter Told You They Wanted To Join.

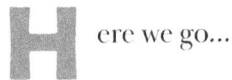ere we go…

MOM INTERVIEW #1. "For years he told me he wanted to go into the Air Force. For his eighteenth birthday, we bought everything to do with the Air Force. I was fine with it because I really didn't think it would happen. I never, at this point, had met with any recruiters. Then one day, I was out to dinner, and I got a call from him asking if I could meet with him and a recruiter… but with the Marines! At that moment, my heart dropped, and I think I stopped breathing for a second. This was getting all too real. A couple days later, for two hours, my son and his recruiting officer sat at my kitchen table. I asked him why the sudden change. He looked at me and said, 'Momma, because the Marines will make me a better man.' Never in all of this life, did I see him smile like that, and it was right then that I knew my first born was making the right choice.

As we handed over his birth certificate and other necessary documents, I think I was in shock. But I felt comfortable because he was still smiling. It was at that time I realized, as a mother, I had done my job with him and he was ready to spread his wings and fly! I felt proud that he loves our country that much, that he is willing to die for it. What an amazing feeling. I, of course, hugged him and cried a bit."

MOM #2. "Well, for me it was different. My sons and I always talked about the Marines because my father was in the Marines, and I was supposed to follow in his footsteps but I waited too long. I didn't make good decisions, and I got pregnant with twins, which ruined my chances to go in. I always told my son stories and about my desire to join.

One day my son and I were talking on the phone. I was at work, and he was telling me how college didn't feel right; like it was not for him and he felt frustrated. So, I asked him where his heart was at, and what he wanted to do. He said he wanted to join the Marines, that all of my stories made him want to join and be a part of that. Since I couldn't, he wanted to. I asked him what he was waiting for, and he said, 'Mom, I hate to leave you, I am worried you will be alone... and if you will be okay.' I told him that I would be fine. I then called the recruiter and asked if we could come in and talk. The recruiter was rude at first, and told me to just have my son call him. I said no! I asked the recruiter if he had a problem speaking face-to-face. He said no, so I told him that we would be there after I got out of work. I felt joy, pride, and excitement that he was going to do what I never did, and failed to do.

I felt so proud that he would follow in my Dad's footsteps, and my Dad would be so proud of him. I may be even a little envious that he is living a dream that I wanted, but failed [to do], only to disappoint my Dad."

Mom #3: "It's amazing how many emotions you can feel at the same time. Pride was the first emotion, but then I was scared and nervous... and excited. I always knew my son wanted to go into the Military (Marines). I would have supported him no matter what!"

Mom #4: "My first thought when he told me he was interested in joining the Air Force was pure joy because, at that time, he was unsure of what direction he wanted to take. My emotions were all over the place because he had been home-schooled since 6th grade, and I had been home with him the entire time. He is my only child, so I was excited, yet scared and nervous."

Mom #5: "Both of my twin boys always said they were going to join the Marines, but when they came home asking for their birth certificates and such, and I was told they were with a recruiter, I was in disbelief. Then came the fear, followed by great pride!"

Mom #6: "At first I was against it, but after seeing what the Marine Corps had to offer, I was excited for her. I had so many emotions – fear, pride, excitement, everything you can imagine."

Mom #7: "My son is in the Marine Corps. He decided at the age of five that he was going to serve. He actually enlisted online at the age of five, and I had recruiters calling me.

After they found out his age, they kept in touch. His junior year, three Marines showed up in uniform to talk to him. I was proud and scared at the same time."

Mom #8: "I was surprised, yet happy that he made the choice to join the Marines. He was only seventeen when he signed up, so his Dad and I had to approve. I was nervous, happy, and worried. I think I felt all the emotions. Overall, I was proud."

INTERVIEW QUESTION 3

"How Has This Changed Your Life?"

Mom #1: "I believe [his] being in the service has changed my life by leaning more on God, and putting it all in His hands. It has also made me learn to trust my son more, and believe that he truly knows what he is doing. It made the house quieter, but I am used to that now. It has given me the chance to really miss him, but to also remember all the great times we had before he left. I'm not going to lie, boot camp was a huge life changer that caused tons of stress and sleepless nights, but I kept telling myself, 'No news is good news, and he is doing what he was destined to do.'"

Mom #2: "At first, it changed my life in the beginning. I traveled a lot, when I never did before. I traveled to go see him [at] all his graduations and just to hang out. It was/is very important to me. I thought it brought us even closer."

Mom #3: "I cry all the time. When I hear the National Anthem, I cry. I have more pride in our country and our service members than I ever knew possible... and I miss him! I get lonely and sad thinking about the times we are missing, but then we get to talk and text, and I know he's right where he should be. He's serving our country!"

Mom #4: "Since my son left for B.M.T., and is now at his first duty station, everything in my life has changed. I am one of those mothers that did everything for him and now, with him not being home, at first I was pretty lost. He has been gone since the beginning of November, and I am getting better. But I worry about him, and I think about him every day."

Mom #5: "I feel like it has changed my life in many different ways. Being That they (my twin boys) are our only children, the house is now empty. Most events and holidays are spent without them. When I shop, I go to grab something they love, and I put it back. That happens a lot. I want to change their rooms to guest rooms, but can't seem to do it. I keep their doors closed (sad face)."

Mom #6: "I have more pride for my country, and definitely pay closer attention to the events happening in the world."

Mom #7: "There was a lot of 'not knowing'. I always tried to be strong so he wouldn't see me worry. There are a lot of sleepless nights."

Mom #8: "I would say that my life didn't change much because my son lived with his Dad. He was already away. The hard part was not being able to talk to him when I wanted, not being able to see him off when he left. That was really hard for me."

INTERVIEW QUESTION 4

What Is Your Favorite
Part About Being A
Military Mom?

Mom #1: "The FaceTime calls mean so much. The sweet gifts that he sends me about his life and whereabouts… But mostly, the other Military Moms I have met through groups! I have new friends that I would have never known if it weren't for him choosing this life path. I have new forever-family, and that is the best thing ever!"

Mom #2: "My favorite part of being a Military Mom is the look of pride on people's faces when I tell them my son is a Marine, and meeting fellow mommas. Also, holding those Welcome Home signs at the airport with so many strangers joining me. I signed up to be a Blue Star Mom in hopes that I can still stay involved somehow."

Mom #3: "The camaraderie that the moms have… that people I have never met in person have my back. We are all connected in this crazy 'Mom' world.

I have made so many friends with other mothers whose children are in the service, and other service members and their families. When people know you have a child in the military, they want to talk, and they want to know about your child. They want to share in your joy… It's amazing!"

Mom #4: "The best part of being a Military Mom for me is the pride that I have for my son. I am beyond proud of him!"

Mom #5: "Definitely the pride! You want to shout it from the top of the highest building, but you don't."

Mom #6: "My favorite part of being a Military Mom is the sense of pride I have for my daughter. I love seeing the look of shock on people's faces when I tell them I have a female Marine!"

Mom #7: "The pride, and knowing that other Military Moms understand what I am going through."

Mom #8: "My favorite part about being a Military Mom is the pride I feel every day, and the online friendships that I have made. It is a unique family. I love being a part of it."

INTERVIEW QUESTION 5

What Is It Like Being A
Military Mom?

The fifth and final question is one that I was most curious about, so I decided to ask several more Military Moms this question, in addition to the eight moms that I had already interviewed.

Mom #1: "For me, being a Military Mom is a true blessing. I am so beyond proud to brag about my Marine. It is also a reminder that I did a good job in raising a hero. It is tough at times, but that is when you lean on your other Military families. I couldn't be happier knowing my son is doing what makes him happy. Military life was a choice my son made, and I am so happy to be a part of it."

Mom #2: "For me, right now, being a Military Mom is tough. My fear is something happening to my son, and not finding out due to family issues."

Mom #3: "It is amazing and heart-breaking at the same time. My son enlisted right out of high school, so we went from having my oldest (only boy) home 24/7 to leaving for boot camp and not living at home anymore. He is now in California. I live in New York State. We do not get very much time to see each other. It's a lot to learn to live with, but he does call and text us. I am proud of him every single day for deciding to join the Marines. I am proud that he decided to stand up and serve!"

Mom #4: "Being a Military Mom to me is a mix of emotions. Besides being proud, I tend to worry on a daily basis if he is doing alright. I worry more these days with everything that is going on in the world we live in, and I can't be there for him at the drop of a dime.

He is stationed on the other side of the country from where I am, so that makes it difficult for me as well, because I just can't hop on a plane and see him whenever I want."

Mom #5: "It feels like a family when you connect with other Military Moms and families. It is a constant feeling of unease. You worry when they say they're feeling unhappy about something and you can't help them change it. Having two boys in the Military doubles the ups and downs. You feel like the Military consumes you because really, it does now. It's your life. You feel proud all of the time. Your kids are actually making a difference, and are the protectors of our country. Things change in their lives in a New York minute, and not always the way they want it to go. Semper Gumby."

Mom #6: "Being a Military Mom is unique. You become bonded with a whole new family you never knew you had. All of the moms support each other's worries and fears."

Mom #7: "It is a lot of sleepless nights, and dealing with people's thoughts/beliefs about the Military having everything handed to them, which they don't. They pay for their gear, food, and supplies. Non-Military Moms tell me they know how I feel because my son is so far away. No, they don't. Only other Military Moms will ever understand."

Mom #8: "Being a Military Mom is one of the most difficult things, but the pride I feel makes it easier. You will never stop worrying, wondering, and hoping for the best. You want them close, but you know that is not always possible."

"What is it like being a Military Mom for you?" These were the responses from the additional Military Moms that I asked: "Super Super proud, but definitely a rollercoaster of emotions. Missing my son so much." "Proud, missing my son." "So proud. Miss my baby, but damn proud." "I am very proud of my son. It's been tough lately because he is on his first deployment." "So, so proud of my daughter for being a Marine, but I miss her so much. The pride I feel for her is nothing I have ever felt before." "I am beyond proud of my son. The rollercoaster ride is and always will be nerve-wracking, but my heart is full of pride." "Humbling. My Daddy served in the Corps in WWII. I have many family members who are veterans, and a few still serving. I'm proud, but mostly humbled. My son told us when he was about eight years old that he was going to be a Marine like Papa.

He never wanted to do anything but be a Marine." "Proud. Like I want to scream it from the rooftops: 'My son is a Marine'! The missing him, and not hearing from him, is like riding a bike that is on fire!" "Super proud of my boys. The ups and downs are real, and missing them like crazy, but besides that, this is what they chose to do. I love them for that sacrifice." "Proud and very humble at the same time. The selfless decision these men/women make is humbling, so much that you can't help but want to try and emanate that. Our kids are a reflection of us, but once they are in the Military, I believe we become a reflection of them when we say we are Military Mamas." "Being a Military Mom is a journey. When I was in, I didn't worry about my parents. I'm sure my Marine isn't worrying about us."

Well, there you have it...the end of the Military Mom interviews. Can you relate to any of these moms? I am so grateful to all of them for shedding light on questions that constantly plagued my mind. I now realize that I am not the only Military Mom that feels so many different emotions all at the same time. Speaking of emotions, it was clear to me that all of these moms shared that one universal emotion... PRIDE! Pride is the one thing that ALL Military Moms have in common. And rightfully so! I mean, really, the Military is only made up of less than one half of 1% of the U.S. population, so how could you not feel that pride that your son/daughter is willing to be part of that 1%? I am sure most of you know, or will know soon, that it is not easy being a Military Mom. In fact, it is probably the hardest thing you will ever do in your life!

Military Moms, hands down, are a breed of their own. They are always there for each other, praying for each other, and helping each other any way they can. I felt that God was calling on me to help as many Military Moms as I could. My Facebook group "Military Mom Life" was one way that I could accomplish that. Another way I did this was by creating t-shirts/apparel for Military Moms to express their pride. You can find them at: www.militarymomlife.org. Last, but not least, I figured that one of the best ways to help Military Moms was to give them advice on how to "survive" their Military Mom journey. Thanks to a bunch of Military Moms! They were willing to give three pieces of advice (or more) to you, and new Military Moms. I hope this advice helps you, and eases some of your doubts and fears. Being a Military Mom is a journey, and I hope I can help you understand it a little better.

ADVICE FOR NEW & VETERAN MILITARY MOMS

I will give you my four pieces of advice first, and will follow with the advice from other Military Moms. Here we go...

1) Send them to boot camp with a pocket-sized notebook. In it, put motivational quotes, Bible quotes, and tell them how much you love them and are proud of them. My son (Marine) said this got him through boot camp, and it helped me to feel connected to him when I couldn't be.

2) Be honest with your son/daughter. They want to be told if a tragedy happens at home (ex. The dog died, Grandma's in the hospital, etc.). They don't want you to "save their feelings," or protect them from bad news. This is coming from my Marine.

3) Move Heaven and Earth if you have to, but make sure you are there to see your child graduate from boot camp/training. They worked hard, and went through unspeakable things. Show them your support and how proud you are of them. They will appreciate it.

4) Do things you enjoy to keep your mind occupied and your stress level down (ex. exercise, meditation, crafts, etc.). It's important that you take care of yourself.

Now you will hear the advice from other Military Moms. Some may be similar, but all great advice! This excellent advice is divided into several categories. The categories are: Communication, Love/Prayers/Support, Sacrifice & Strength, Pride/Self-Reflection/Gratitude, Family & Friends, and Education.

COMMUNICATION

Communication is everything, and it comes in all different forms. Most moms were aligned with the statement "No news is good news." Sue says, "Write, write, write when your child is at boot camp. They need it, and it is so very helpful. Keep the lines of communication open. Send care packages if possible. They love homemade cookies and goodies. Remember, they are still your babies no matter what!" Linda gives similar advice, as she says, "Write them, send them packages, text them, call them and leave messages. They love getting stuff from home." Jessica says, "Don't speak negative of your child's command or branch. Keep it positive, and if something happens (and it can wait until he gets home), keep it to yourself because their heads need to be where they are." Sharon and Barb have similar advice. They say, "Don't question them to death, and don't harp on things and tell them what to do."

Amy says, "Never say 'Goodbye'; it's 'See you later'." "Always tell them how proud you are of them," Cindy. The last piece of advice for communication comes from Anna, and that is, "Be supportive and always listen to their good news and reply with praise. Listen to their complaints, and reply with encouraging words."

LOVE/PRAYERS/SUPPORT

There is nothing more important than love, prayers, and support for your child! Sue advises, "Always be encouraging them; they are going through so much. Even when they get out of boot camp and go to their next training, until they are working at their jobs. They need so much love, understanding, and encouragement. This is not about you – this is about them. They need your love and support." Liz, Monica, and Amanda all give similar advice. They say, "Be supportive through good and bad, and pray, pray, pray. It's hard on you but it's hard on them as well. They may come home and act different, and you might not be used to that, but just understand that they have changed a lot, and may not be the same boy you sent away. It is also important to be supportive if your child is sent out on a medical discharge (this happened to me). Transition is hard. Be there for your child, but don't smother them. They have a lot to figure out."

Sharon feels it is so important to always say 'I love you.' Jessica, Tiffany, and Katelynn say, "Support and find any and every way you can to keep in touch. Send them mail often, no matter how frequently you talk... and send their roommate a little sumthin' sumthin' in the package too. After boot camp, send care packages as often as possible. Homemade treats usually get you a photo, or even a phone call home." Lauren says to pray Psalm 91 over him! Alison and Ashley say, "Trust God, always pray, and be supportive of your child. Be flexible and just love." This next one is from Robyn: "Trust me, they are missing you and home just as much as you are missing them. Make sure to keep it positive when writing. Send cards, dad jokes, and pictures."

Barb and Donna say, "Keep your phone close, so when they reach out to you, you are prepared to listen." According to Deanna, "Always, always tell them you love and miss them, you are proud of them, and to stay safe." Kelly gives some important advice for all of you Military Moms. She says, "As a mom, you need to hold yourself together in order to support them (it's a bumpy ride)... and have the couch ready when they come home; that's

SACRIFICE & STRENGTH

When your child is in the Military, not only do they make sacrifices, but so do you! Being a Military Mom requires a whole lot of strength... You got this!

Nancy feels it is necessary to "Remind yourself daily that this is what your child chose to do, and it is making them happy. Sit back and enjoy watching them soar. Lean on God and pray! Enjoy every text or FaceTime call you receive... and when you get to hug them, hold on until you just can't anymore." Mary says, "Boot camp or any basic training is tough to get through, but you do. Hold on because your ride will be crazy for the next 4 years. There are ups and downs, that is why *Military Mom Life* is a great group to be a part of." Anna and Tiffany have similar advice: "When they come home to visit, let them dictate what they want to do. You are missing one person, he/she is missing their whole pre-Military life."

Sometimes they just want to be alone and decompress. Other times, they want to be out all day with their friends. They will always need mom. Be patient while they are establishing adulthood." Molly says, "Be stronger when he/she isn't." Sharon and Cara's advice is "Semper Gumby is your friend. Be okay for plans and trips to change or get postponed at the last minute. Try not to get your hopes up of them coming home, until you are face-to-face with your child."

PRIDE/SELF-REFLECTION/GRATITUDE

The amount of pride you feel as a Military Mom is indescribable! Becoming a Military Mom changes you as a person... You discover things you never knew about yourself, and you appreciate the things you never even thought about before your child entered the Military. Donna, Cindy, and Nina feel the same. They say, "Stay strong, be positive, and be patient. You will have good days, really good days, bad days, and really bad days. Remember, your son/daughter is a lot stronger than you think." Barb says, "Always keep them in your thoughts (obviously), but don't dwell. Just love them from where they are. They are growing into fine young men and women, and we need to embrace the journey from afar, wherever that is, and as much as that stings."

Janessa and Amy feel that you should "Let the tears flow, and focus on self-care, but treasure the little moments – quick hellos and snapshots of their lives." Robyn says, "Before they leave, tell them in the first letter they write to you, to say where they stand in formation. Also, who is in the front of them, next to them, and behind them. This will make it easier to find them in pictures." Kelly's great advice is, "Even if they are far, make them a part of your every day. For example, we keep mine up to date in Snapchat. He's already missing so much family time, but we make him feel like he is here." Amanda says, "Go to boot camp graduation. It was the most special time for me. I still remember every emotion I felt that day." "Give it all to God because without Him, none of us or any of our boots would get through this crazy life," says Deanna. Linda wants you to "Realize that you are never alone in anything that you feel. All of us moms have gone through it at some point, and we are here to support each other!"

FAMILY & FRIENDS

As you know, family and friends are such an integral part of our lives. They help and support us in countless ways. Although they are missing your child too, they will never understand how you feel, and what you are truly going through... and they shouldn't because only another Military Mom has that capability and privilege.

Robyn says, "You are NEVER ALONE HERE. We are all different, but we are Family, and we stand together! Emotions can run high, so be considerate of others." Amanda feels that it is a good idea to "Find online support groups. They have been so helpful to me. I also found it helpful to follow my son's Base on Facebook. I can see some things that are going on there, and it helps. There are the boot camp groups also. I was able to look online to see photos while he was at boot camp."

Deanna says, "Make it known to family when your boots come home that your door is open. Family can come to them; they shouldn't spend leave-time traveling and having to stress about going to see people. They did their part of traveling by coming home." I am going to interject here. I whole-heartedly agree with Deanna. I witnessed this first-hand when my son came home on leave. He was very stressed out because he felt like he had to visit as many family members as he could, and all he wanted to do was to relax. The last thing your son/daughter needs when they come home is to be stressed out! Their home is their safe haven, and they deserve to do what they want when they come, not to stress out.

Mary says, "Definitely join different groups on Facebook or other social media. It helps, and you can make great friends. No one understands what you are going through when you have a kid in the Military... unless they have one in there too." This last one is from Linda, and I'm sure most of you have experienced this (or will experience it). I know I have! Linda says, "People that do not have kids in the Military will compare their kid to yours. Going to college is NOTHING like going into the Military. It is just not worth the argument!"

EDUCATION

Your child is in the Military now, and with that comes a whole bunch of questions and concerns. Educate yourself the best you can. Every branch of the Military is different, and has different rules and regulations. Knowledge is power!

Amy and Liz say, "Never say where they are or where they are traveling too, but stay alert and aware of what is going on in the world." Jessica feels that it is important to learn everything you can about your child's branch, and to take everything you hear with a grain of salt. She recommends that you don't go to your son/daughter's command about an issue... Let them do it. Teresa says, "Don't expect details. Learn to be happy with a simple conversation." Katelynn feels that you should always buy the travel insurance any time you plan on visiting your child. The Military is known for changing their plans at the last minute, so you may have to cancel your trip. The travel insurance will allow you to be reimbursed.

There is no doubt that being a Military Mom comes with countless and unprecedented emotions. What you may be feeling or going through may be the same as another Military Mom, however, you may handle or deal with your emotions differently than those moms. The key to surviving your journey as a Military Mom is to acknowledge your feelings and realize that you may react to certain things in ways you never thought you would. That is okay! So what if you cry when you hear the National Anthem... Cut yourself some slack. You have taken on a new role in your life, and it is not easy. I hope that the advice from these moms helps you along your Military Mom journey, and that you take pride and comfort in knowing that we are all here for each other. Take it one day at a time, and do whatever you have to do to keep yourself healthy and sane, so that you can do your job as a Military Mom and support your child. Never forget that you are brave, courageous, and stronger than you think! Just as your son/daughter was called on to serve our great country, so were you. You got this, and whether you believe it or not, you were made for this! Best of wishes to you along your Military Mom life journey. "We are stronger together, cuz we're in it together!"

Joshua 1:9

Be strong and courageous. Do not be afraid, do
Not be discouraged, for the lord your god will
Be with you wherever you go.

Psalm 144:1

Blessed be the lord, my rock, who trains my
Hands for war, and my fingers for battle.

John 15:13

Greater love has no one than this that someone lay down his life for his friends.

Psalm 91

Thank you that i can dwell in your shelter and rest in the
Shadow of your almighty power and strength.
I can confidently say that you are my refuge and my fortress.
You are my god, in whom I trust. I ask that you will save me
from the fowler's snare, and from the deadly pestilence
that swirls around me.
I trust that you will cover me with your feathers, and
under your wings i will find refuge.
Your faithfulness is my shield and rampart.
I will not fear the terror of night, nor the arrow that flies
by day, nor the pestilence that stalks in the darkness,
nor the plague that destroys at midday.
A thousand may fall at my side, ten thousand at my
right hand, but it will not come near me.
I will only observe with my eyes and see the
punishment of the wicked.
Thank you for being my Refuge.
You are the most high and you are my dwelling.
No harm will overtake me, and no disaster will come near my tent.
I pray this in your name, amen.

ABOUT THE AUTHOR

Tracey D'Amore went from an average mom to a Military Mom in 2017. She is the mom of a Marine and an Airman. Tracey was not prepared to be a Military Mom, and because this was going to be a real thing, she had to prepare herself. Like any new Military Mom, Tracey had no idea what to expect, and was filled with fear and anxiety. She could not understand why her two boys would want to put themselves in harm's way and join the military. Tracey has been teaching for 26 years, and has a Master's degree in education. She has always been active in her children's lives. Her concern of how to cope with all the emotions of being a Military Mom led her to start her Facebook group "Military Mom Life," and to write *The Mind Of A Military Mom-Military Moms' Advice on How To Survive Being A Military Mom*. Tracey's goal is to help as many Military Moms as she can while are on their Military Mom journey, by giving them advice, support, and understanding. Tracey's motto is... "We're Stronger Together, Cuz We're In It Together"!

⌐ SUPPORT ¬

Don't let this be the end of our journey together.
Join us in our Facebook group:

- Military Mom Life -

We brag, we support each other, we share what's on our minds, we can be ourselves, and we are one of the only Facebook groups that accepts Military Moms of all branches of the military
(Army, Navy, Air Force, Marines, Coast Guard)!
Can't wait to meet you in person!

Also, like us and follow us on Instagram at:

military_mom_life

APPAREL

That's right... Apparel!

You are not just a mom, you are a Military Mom! All Military Moms should be able to express their pride of being a Military Mom.

Check out Military Mom Life's Apparel...

www.militarymomlife.org

"Be Proud... Wear Your Pride!"

Made in United States
North Haven, CT
14 June 2025